by Edward Dorn

Poetry

The Newly Fallen (1961)
Hands Up! (1964)
Geography (1965)
Idaho Out (1965)
North Atlantic Turbine (1967)
Twenty-Four Love Songs (1969)
Songs Set Two—A Short Count (1970)
Recollections of Gran Apacheria (1973)
Collected Poems (1975)
Manchester Square (with Jennifer Dorn) (1976)
Hello, La Jolla (1978)
Yellow Lola (1981)
Captain Jack's Chaps (1983)
Gunslinger (1989)
Abhorrences (1990)

Prose

The Rites of Passage (1971)
    (revised later as By the Sound)
Some Business Recently Transacted in the White World (1971)

Nonfiction

The Shoshoneans (1966)
    (with photographs by Leroy Lucas)

Translations (with Gordon Brotherston)

The Tree Between Two Walls (1969)
Our Word (1968)
Cesar Vallejo Selected Poems (1975)

ABHORRENCES

EDWARD
DORN

BLACK SPARROW PRESS ▶◀ SANTA ROSA ▶ 1990

Acknowledgments

Some of these poems first appeared in the following publications: *Conjunctions, Intent, Rolling Stock, White Cloud Review, Willow Springs, Zephyr.* "Aid(e) Memoire," "The Ed Meese Scrolls," "Not So Hard Wired, but Something to Do" and "World View Solipsized" were published as a Silver Buckle broadside; "Welcome Home" was published as a broadside by the Friends of the Library and the Black Mountain Collection of North Carolina Wesleyan College; "Ode on the Facelifting of the 'statue' of Libery" was published by Louisiana State University Press; and "Another Springtime in the Rockies," "Martyrs Opera," "Progress: slow but inexorable," "Don't just stand there, get something!" and "Thou shalt Not Kill: Oh Yes I Will" appeared in a Limberlost Press (Boise) chapbook.

Black Sparrow Press books are printed on acid-free paper.

LIBRARY OF CONGRESS CATALOGING-IN-PUBLICATION DATA

Dorn, Edward.
    Abhorrences / Edward Dorn.
        p.   cm.
ISBN 0-87685-801-9 : — ISBN 0-87685-802-7 (hard, signed)
: — ISBN 0-87685-800-0 (pbk.) :
    I. Title.
PS3507.073277A67   1990
811'.54—dc20

90-34816
CIP

for Jennifer Dunbar Dorn

Table of Contents

ABHORRENCES
A Chronicle of the Eighties

A B H O R R E N C E S : Baseline Vocabulary introduced by the Rawhide Era

Here we go again

PROGRESSIVITY
ASSASSINALITY
INVÃDITUDE
OVERTHROWISM
FREEDUMNESS
OLIGARCHARIANISM
CONTRAMENTALITY
RIGHT-WING TO LIFE
MEESAGOGUERY

HELICOPTERY
NUCLEARSUBERY
NUCLEARSHRUBBERY
DEMOBUGGERY
PLACEKICKERY
South Affery
FOODSHIPMENT
AIRFORCEONEERY
GUNSHIPICIDE

LANDSLIDICIDE
BLASTOFFIC
AVALANCHERY
COUNTRYCIDE
RIVERCIDE
RAWHIDE
MOTELERY

STRONGARMISIMO
CANALERY
PLATINUMBLONDAGE
PUDENDUMONY
FUNNYMONEY
GRAND OLE GHOULICANS
HAPPYSLAPPERY
OPTIMOSTERY
PLENTYTUDE
RUDE&NUDE

NEBRASKACIDE
ONEUMVIRATES
FIELDGHOULS
GHASTLITUDES
HIGHNOONISM
LAUNCHINGPADITUDE

REABORTIONMENT
GAYETY
ASSKICKERY
BUSHERY
ARTILLERY
MIDNIGHT BOWLING, the
   protestant answer to bingo
DEEP COMA AROMA
HOLLYWOODEN

■

Print the invasion money

■

one bullet
is worth
a thousand bulletins

ABHORRENCES
Motto, 9th decade

■

Every Man
for Herself.

Never Lose an Enemy,
if you can help it

On capturing the disapproval
of the fat goose
with the baked potato for a nose
spasms of laughter and contemplation
surged through my peptide chains.

ABHORRENCES
Motto

Los Ochentas

No porn
to speak of
but filth
by the
boatload

The Protestant View:

that eternal dissent
and the ravages of
faction are preferable
to the voluntary
servitude of blind
obedience.

Generic Eighties

Anything you can push,
pull,
or tow in.

While You're at it

As long as you're closing The Window of Vulnerability
would you mind shutting that door of paranoia
And while you're at it, would you mind
sweeping the carpet of disdain.
And then there's the container of trash to carry out
When you're finished with that
you might go to the kitchen where you'll find
the skillet of rashness. Uh,
just throw in a few slices of the bacon of compatibility
and fry well.

Wait Till the Christians
Hear About This!

In his effort to get prayer into the schools
President Reagan reminded us
that the ancient Romans and Greeks fell
when they abandoned their gods:
students needn't "pray" exactly,
for instance, they might "think"
for a while before school starts.

If he means that, Thought could get
the biggest boost it's had for years.
Maybe they could think about some greek myths.
And what about sacrifices?
I wouldn't mind seeing Cap Weinberger on a spit.
Maybe they could consider the Aztecs—
I wouldn't mind at all
seeing Jeanne Kirkpatrick's frosty heart
raised to the heathen skies.

Not Good, but Getting Better:
dog fights on the increase in Denver.

It would have been as good to live
with Genghis Khan as Reagan Ron,
with the mass decapitations of Khorasan,
the garden of Asia
as the industrial strength genocides
in the gardens of Missouri.
Remember the town
that had to be scraped off—villa dioxin.
It's just dog shit—a society of hi-tek dogshit.

Apocryphal or not . . .

One of Boulder's sleazier restaurants
had a customer this summer
who could perhaps best
be described as a literalist:
he appeared for dinner wearing *only*
a shirt and a pair of shoes.

The Vulgarity of Positive Reinforcement
or Putting Away Childish Things

(for T.C.

When I received my first doses
of surprising praise
I was thrilled to the bone
and reviewed their every angle
time and time again
until exhaustion with it
made me grow weary.

Stronger praise, and a certain devotion
followed like a decimated army of lemmings
but my expectations were now hard to satisfy
and thoughts of suspicion and real revenge
lay like a weight in me when praise was weak
or qualified by considerations
I had distinctly accounted for in my system.

But all that seems immature
and superficial, now that I've felt
the bite of hate, dread and envy
passions much truer than mere admiration
and always more honest.

Casting the First Puffball

Moral bankruptcy
is no great charge
at a time when
plastic morality
can be avoided
only with $20 gold pieces
and *they* aren't in circulation.

A Decision Taken with Little Thought and Even Less Pain

I want to hear power.
Big, smooth,
twelve cylinder power.

I want to hear sandstone
intelligence
on the dull edge of truth.

And voices that don't inflect
the slightest fiction
of fairmindedness.

So I turned off All Things Considered.

Flatland

People make a lot of fun
of the Flat Earthers,
but the fact is,
in a lot of places
the earth is flat.

Lemma Japonaise

The speculating economist asks
as if by asking himself he asks
all mankind, Will we, as a society
be able to keep up with Japan.
Sometimes, there is nothing
so demented as the rhetorical.

Nevertheless, Do we even want
to live in a beehive culture,
worker bees confecting chips which
turn out robots turning out robots.

A glance at this scene shows
we've already done that.
Instead of banning books,
those fools out in the stix
would better serve their goofy progeny
by banning walkman.

Rough Passage on I-80

We are travelling through the country
where "Thank you Oh Lord
for the deal I'm about to receive"
is chiselled into the blacktop
like a crow's incantation.

It's minus 3 degrees
on the Count Fahrenheit scale.
It would be Boraxo country
except there ain't no Boraxo.
And no mule teams. Here the mules drive.

Those rolling hills out there
are full of coal and oel and moly
a lota moly, that's lybdenum
the kind of denum the cowboys
around here wear. Around here everybody's
a cowboy with no cows
and every cow is without boys.
The boys have all gone to Rock Springs
to drill and to get shot.

Low trailers hunkered in the Winde,
the big snau-blower. Scrap rock, like deinosaur fins
strung along the saurian freeway. Ah,

to endeavor to gain what another endeavors
to gain at the same time — competition!
eight barrelled, sharp clawed!

The graft is longbed style, Shot the Sheriff
fur shure, plus some shot the D.A. types,
they're all here. Tractor hat Stranglers,
Drive-up Drinkers, Mobile Snorters,
Pass on the Right Siders — mega rednek,
and for good reason — they've lynched all the Lavender Neks.
More dangerous than Beirut.
They don't take hostages,
they don't take anything alive.

White rock faces, Four-Wheelers,
Big Dealers, Slim Jim Peelers,
Teased Hair Squealers! YaaHoo!
beller the Yahoos, it's where
they make the springs rock —
they don't call it Rock Springs for nothin'.

RADIO: White Christmas scrap,
Der Bingle baritone in motheaten night-cap.
We see through the landscape:
black rubbermaid crows
sail past a turquoise trailer, cold aluminum
hunched under the guns of the winde.
Inside the sleeping resident turns
on a couch of budweiser cans
lips frozen turquoise, wrenched,
limbs on the pike to gangrene.

RADIO MUSAK: Gordon Lightleg!
dulcimerland, vests on pennywhistles,
Folkak, Blusak, Rucksak Rock.

On to Rollins and Riggins.
Steel mosquitoes probe an oel poule.
Deinosaur blood, black and crude,
the awful, devious oleo-olfactory

death odour, atomic weight 32, low and volatile,
driven by the pistons of hell,
the transfusion of the red roadmap,
where those stumping bags of the autoperiod
were once given to roam. Out the window
the Prontosauris Oil Company
sits next to the Horny-toed Boot Factory,
Overthrust Belt getting looser and looser now
after the gas these "Big Boys with popcorn teeth"
sucked out of the mantle.

On the asphalt cinch, rolling along,
kidneybelts tightened, the Kenworth Tractorsaurus
stampede into Wamsutter, Lusk, Dittlebone
and other such turquoise-eye-shadow towns.

The Wamsutter Hotel is totally electric.
Gas, permanent vacancy,
Conoco, Amoco, nowhere to go.
That Big Trailer over there
is where the Mayor lives,
pole light on all night,
prowling dogs, cringe and slobber
for an ankle to crush—not the friend of Everyman.
All this would be on a hill but there ain't none.

Gay Johnson installations
on both sides of the Strip.
The Howard Johnson of the High West.
A woman built like a stack of tires
fills up her coupé—SIGN
"Gay Johnsons, Buses Invited, Tobacco."
On second thought, Howard Johnson
doesn't deserve
to be the Gay Johnson of Wyoming.

Roadkill scattered like throwrugs
on blacktop. All the groundrunners
are either smart (located elsewhere)
or dead at the wheels of the heavy hitters.

Speedy schools of pickup trucks
scatter ahead of hunter packs of tractorsaurus,
Terribledactyl birds,
ghosts of old clavichord players
swoop with heavy grecian wings
to snatch up flat rabbit fleeces
from the altar of the tar, Wyoming crêpes
dredged in pea-gravel crude.

RADIO: Governor of Wyoming Safety Bulletin:
Recommends strapping skis bottomup
on roof-rack in case of flip-over.
Woman held in tract house by unidentified
Gillette Krak Dealer — across town six onlookers
killed when police check out false report
and man rains lead on the unpaved avenue.

    State Trooper ahead between the strips,
coffee thermos in officer's fist.
His police shield doubles as Rad Badge of Courage.
Snow fences, like arthritic twigs of protozoa
vanish into the vale of snow — the world is getting colder
as the transmitted propaganda says it is getting warmer.

TRANSMISSION FROM GILLETTE: The Razor City.
Serious roadkill this time — they're digging with backhoes
and throwing the victims in.
Gillette: people have been known
to go there just to have their throats cut.
AD: "Trucker's Mistress,"
a truckstop item hooked to cigarette lighter
with concertina wire stretching to vitals
for over-the-road Mechanical Head —
available in truckstop gift shops
with Chain Wallets and Turquoise Buckles —
"A real herpie saver."

    Laramie exits flash by like marked cards.
University of Wyo. What do they teachem there?
Nothin' works with ranchin' anyhay these days.

There they go, canterin' to the subcafeteria
in search of teflon heffers. Say!
What do you do when a Wyoming Cowboy
throws you a pin? Run like Hell!
because the grenade in his mouth
is about to go off!

   Willie's on again . . .
all the truckertops and lesser heavy hitters
singing along under parts-shop, feedstore web hats,
the houseflies washed out in the strenuous amphetewake.
"On the Rode Again. . . ."
Three Hundred pound Choir Boys
with eyes like strawberry-coconut donuts.

Crawling to Little America in Cheyenne.
Twenty-six degrees below Count Fahrenheit.
The transmission from Gillette fallen silent.
Cut off by the authorities no doubt. Somebody asks
how interesting can a town afford to be?
The soft, reasonable talk of Denver
supplants the airwaves, the jittery compromise of the city
crowds out the spontaneous stix.

   A yellow ivory ball of pollution
hangs above Cheyenne's fibreglass air.
The Santa Claus-bright Gettysaurus Reks Refinery
is strewn along our approach, blowing
not so symbolic mushrooms, MX Missile Burgers,
the biggest meat in Strip Town.

Martyrs are a dime a dozen around here.
The best ones have been dead a long time.

ABHORRENCES
1984, February 1st

Homo Sap:

What could be more predictable
than that the great Teller does not
accept the theory of a nuclear winter,
and that furthermore He speculates
the earth might get hotter—
a sort of broadened Florida,
all the way to Labrador, like it used to be.
These people always did prefer Hell—
the Faustian Bargain on a Brechtian stage,
a fire sale in a furniture Dome.

Boulder Mundane

It is all very continuous here.
The temper has been like enamel
For a straight week—
A kind of Kracking Dry Bite,
The best selling Japanese breakfast food
Emitting the heat of a photograph.
We're living in a picture of reality.
The joggers stop-frame down the street.
Birds are caught in wingspread
And never reach the roof.
The only things changing here
Are the traffic lights.
Another Kopy Shoppe opens.
This is a town obsessed with reproduction,
But few babies are born.

World View Solipsized

The oecologists now say
creatures are eligible for survival
if they have no inbuilt yen
for human flesh.
That's a legitimate,
self-interested position.
But it would have no standing
among the insects.

The Ed Meese Scrolls

Kicking Ed Meese
is like kicking a toadstool.
No "my fellow citizens"
Ed Meese is not the problem.
The stoolies on Capitol Hill
want this loyal fan of the police
for Attorney General so desperately
acceptance would be hard to hide.
What's this talk of tradition?
This *is* the tradition.

Not So Hard Wired, but something to do

Recusants who never wrote
a damn line in their smug lives
or even divided a pie
or if they had a thought
couldn't get it out
with a corkscrew,
Now regularly bathe
in the gangrene glow
of Crosstalk and Smartcom
like a herd of gallsick cattle.

Aid(e) Memoire

If you screw
and are screwed by
everybody you meet
24 hours a day
every day of the year
you'll get a disease
as we learn from the History of the Renaissance.
So why not forego
the gamble and drink
directly from the sewer.

Spring, 1984
Giv'em the sack
& raise their rent

Smoke & Cinders:
Some Thoughts on the Truckers

Every time I hear the dispatches
of shock and dismay
over the violence of labor,
it's clear who owns the radio.

Capitalism was founded
on cracked heads and broken ribs
and machine gunning.
No need to invoke Ludlow.
No need to bring up Homestead.
The violence is too widespread
to be symbolized by one or two
situations past or present.

And *capitalism*, from such barbarity,
has come to be sanctified most
by those who deplore the violence of labor.

I wonder,
do they have some *other* model
for the brutes?

Touring the Bloated Void

Why is it the uninterrupted brutalities
maintaining the castes in India
draw hardly a glance, or that
the Calcutta traffic
in live human kidney to the Arabs
merits not a chuckle or mention
from the people who are so shocked
by apartheid?

I'll never apologize again!

"In the so-called aporetic dialogues
various opinions elicited from the respondent
can be reduced to apparent self-contradiction
by the device of getting each of them
reworded in terms of the questioner's
own principles."

(from Eric Havelock)

Ice is the lead of water's gold

And then the shuttle became
a big-scale colostomy bag.
No matter how high the techno perch
plumbing still rules the roost.

Recette Economique

I've always found much
to recommend
in the slogan "Soak the Rich"
but I've never found
much discussion regarding
the uses of that marinade.
I have one modest proposal:
feed them to the poor.

Armalite Resolution

I'm not going to be
a martyr to politeness anymore.

When I see someone with a slight cold
it's the other direction for me.

Self Criticism

I accept the present emperium
for my own, individual good.
I have been striving to become miserly
in all I think and do so that I,
and those few who look to me
for their protection, shall not
be alienated through my recalcitrance.
And I will not be tempted to consider avariciousness wretched,
I shall not wince or shudder
at happy talk, for even as I know it is vapid
and inane, still it is better that its users
be spared the dark tribulations
which might otherwise occupy their consciences
and distract them from their self-righteousness.
And I promise not to consider self-righteousness
in the old, aloof and superior way
which was formerly my wont.

I know that abortion is wrong
and should be shunned
and I shall banish from my mind
the scenes of infanticide
which are condoned the world over
for the good of subject states.
But those questions, again,
I will make myself reluctant to contemplate.

I will approve of genocide in Central America
because it is proprietary
and conforms with our government's policy.
I approve of the reluctant delivery of food
to Ethiopia's starving millions

because that country has a Marxist government
and I agree that magnanimity
in such a situation would be mistaken.
But above all, I am in agreement
with all my government does
because to think otherwise
would be to make of myself an enemy of the state.

When concertina wire is strung along my street
I shall not object, nor will it disturb me
because I am now convinced
that what I formerly took to be
a restriction of my spirit
is in reality, for my salvation,
if salvation is in my future,
but even that doubt is a sign of my humility.

A B H O R R E N C E S
November 5, 1984
From a conversation
with George Kimball
when he was in Denver
with the Patriots

Tuesday was a Fait Accompli, *not a Raison d'Etre:* an election scare story

My friend George has a theory
that the Handlers can prop old Rawhide up
for two years and a day,
declare him unfit, then *Bushery*
until January 1997,
all in conformity with the Roosevelt Rule.

That's a bit pessimistic for my taste.
So I argued the real precedents
were Wilson and Harding—
to wit, drooling collapse and senility
where the wife bluffs it out.
Nancy would certainly consent to that.

But again, as George pointed out,
in those prior examples there was still
an interest in maintaining
the honor of the office—whereas now
Ideology is all.

There's only one natural death,
and even that's Bedcide
For the post-mortem amusement of Richard Brautigan

Death by over-seasoning: Herbicide
Death by annoyance: Pesticide
Death by suffocation: Carbon monoxide
Death by burning: Firecide
Death by falling: Cliffcide
Death by hiking: Trailcide
Death by camping: Campcide
Death by drowning: Rivercide
                        Lakecide
                        Oceancide
Death from puking: Curbcide
Death from boredom: Hearthcide
Death at the hands of the medical profession: Dockcide
Death from an overnight stay: Inncide
Death by surprise: Backcide
Death by blow to the head: Upcide
Death from delirious voting: Rightcide
Death from hounding: Leftcide
Death through war: Theircide & Ourcide
Death by penalty: Offcide
Death following a decision: Decide

It Could be Anyone

It is total nonsense
that if it looks like a duck
walks like a duck,
talks like a duck
swims like a duck
fucks like a duck
it is a duck.
It could be the guy next door.

The Price is Right: A Torture Wheel of Fortune

The show did not start off
auspiciously, the contestants
were nervous and kept fiddling
with the wires attached
to their privates, the men
being especially anxious
over the question of balls.
The women were more querulous.

The first question, a medical subject,
was why had the anti-abortionists
not mentioned, let alone commented on,
the Baboon Heart transplant?
One terrified contestant guessed
it was because the moral majority's
nervous concern with evolution
precluded their bringing it up.
That hopeful contestant's face
reflected the malicious light
in the eyes of the host who
immediately *threw the switch.*

A powerful surge shot through
the wires and both sexes screamed
and writhed, to the delight of
the vast viewership, estimated
at 100 million, all of whom,
presumably, were delighted
not to be on the show,
because not one in a million
knew the answer.

The Wisconsin Hunters to the Chippewas

Now, if you eat Kentucky Fried Chicken
you can't be indian and civilized too.

Now, the poles and the italians
have kept their culture.

You don't need *no* reservation
to maintain your culture.

Now, you never did learn to work,
and the way things turned out
you could have been hunted down
and exterminated.

Which didn't happen entirely
but which some people wanted.

You don't own these deers
any more than anybody else

and we think all those treaties
which *we* didn't make,

have got to be abergated.

Worse than Tapeworm

Nixon was dark
among the moderns.
He suffered a crushing,
massive overdose
of audience. There was
actually no gate on the water.
His rehabilitation was hydroponic
and took up far more, far more
than fifteen minutes—his case
recurs and recurs
as the uncontrollable parasite
in the stomach of the republicans,
the germ of the grocer caste—
much more the counterpoint of Thatcher
than the actor
who, had he been a lawyer,
would have paid off
the body of the host
instead of feeding on it
until it was gone, and there was no more
and the end was never to be known
because the exploiter and the exploited
entered oblivion together.

Homage to Karen Carpenter

Starvation is not
the exclusive privilege
of Africa & India.
There are higher forms of it
and greater refinements
in our own greedy nation.
She was right to die for her image
haunted by the memory
of her lyrical power.

No post mortem warnings
about hazard diets
will change any of that.

Products which are absolutely simple to despise in our state

The use of the word I Go
to express I Said
when relating a response.

Running shoes
with Launching Platform soles.

Fat homosapiens pushing carts
and trust funds for retired chimps.

Grown men dressed in short pants
when Esprit is out of the question.

The use of the weak interjective OK
to mean this is an explanation.

In academia, saying She got her PhD
when the pronoun is entirely inappropriate.

People who say If I don't do it by Tuesday
I'll be sick, when they're sick already.

Small automobiles and apes who drink from cups
while driving to work or walking down hallways.

But most of all shakers who say
I'm Outa Here when they haven't even left.

He spits, therefore he is spittle

Of course, all futures are loaded.
The Eighties will be seen
as the last bit of paradise
hoving out of view:
the opportunities for truly im-
mense fraud, the widespread
cupidity in the appreciation
of contrasts—"Have, Havenot."
These will seem The last of the dream,
a beacon of magnitude
in the acres of time.

Novels Somebody With Nothing To Do Should Write

The Long Breakfast
The Long Lunch
The Long Hello
The Long Nice Day
The Long So Long

Evaporation as a career

She should have a black hat
glued to her head

She already has a Ricky Lee Jones tape
stuck in her cassette.

Logical Appointments: or giving the People what they want by way of giving them what they deserve

What do you do
if you have total contempt for organized labor?
Appoint a racketeer as Secretary of Labor.

What do you do
if you think the law should be for your own convenience?
Appoint a former cop as Attorney General.

What do you do about Foreign Affairs
if you consider the world a big franchise?
Appoint a president of Bechtel Corporation
as Secretary of State,
ditto Secretary of Defense.

What do you do
if you consider land-jobbing & foreclosure
the best medicine for agriculture?
Appoint a man who owns a fair amount of Illinois
and wants the rest of it
to Secretary of Agriculture.

And What do you do
when you're negotiating an arms treaty?
Well, obviously, you appoint a man
who used to be a lobbyist for Lockheed.

ABHORRENCES
Whatever happened
to the Turk? And the
theory he was hired
by the Russians.
28 March, 1985

The Turk

Leading off with a statement
like "I am Jesus Christ,"
was perhaps a bit strong.
Nevertheless, if Jesus Christ
were to return to Earth,
He'd shoot the Pope.

ABHORRENCES
A "found" abhorrence
1 April, 1985

■

"Why is wanting to kill Ronald Reagon
and fuck Jody Foster
considered insane?
Makes sense to me."

(from 2nd floor toilet
Hellems, U.C. Boulder,
by a philosophy student
I would imagine)

Another Springtime in the Rockies

(for P.M.

I called up to see
If I could make a citizen's
Arrest on the telephone —
There were about a thousand people
I wanted to arrest that day.
The answer was No Dice.

Then I called up to see if
I could get arrested on the telephone
For demonstrating against
The C.I.A. because I didn't
have time to go down
to get printed & mugged.
The answer was No Way.

How's that for freedom
And what does it say about
Our highly touted & deregulated
Communications system?

The Calendar Girl at Eddie's

Sheer Silver Pants
sparkling like water
over Perfect Animal falls
fine boned feet
in glass heels,
superbly airbrushed rear detail
strawstack hair fresh from the haystack.
Just now returned from Bangkock
with a load of Batik beds.

Weather Report

Golfball size hail
reported in Littleton.
There are those of us
who have been to Littleton,
and could wish
it'd been soccerball size.

Something we can all agree on

Suppose there were a new
acronym for an old disease —
very awful and very incurable.
Let's call it HELPS for
   Heritable Endemic Longrange
      Poverty Syndrome

Now here's the question:
do you think there would be
much tea & sympathy for this plague?
Neither do I.

These Times Are Medieval

They'd just as soon sell ya
a poison pizza as look atcha.

They'd jusas soon fireya
as hireya

And they'd rather
killya than feedya.

Foreign Policy; another cheap import

Shamir says we agree
and have common aims.
Well Fuck Him,
I didn't vote for
the son-of-a-bitch.
He looks like the mayor
of the planet of the apes.
Why not let North Korea
do our middle east policy?
It wld be cheaper
and better made.

Pow-Wow in Geneva

Stock market up 8 points.
Does that mean
the speculators smell war?
Or that the capitalists are
just on another optimism binge?

I like a Busy View

Framed in the french doors
shut tight against
the anti-therms
evaporate the cuttlebone snows.
Along the barrel of Broadway
rifle compact cars
the next-to-the-next-to-the-last dashboard,
new master of destiny —
the program that
stands in for the tube
during the commute.

Across that perilous divide
the Greeks in their big tatty houses
hold endless tupperware orgies
with soft punk junk.
Quivering over it all, the Great
up-tilted permian slabs
who measure Travel Time in aeons
who consider carbon mono
just a passing gas, and ozone holes
letting the sunshine in.

America, really, No Kidding, the Beautiful.

It's music on your radio,
and it's merry merry Christmas baby
you shure did treat me nice— yea well
I'm feelin mighty fine, music on my radio
but I can't really kiss you baby
becauze your saliva is undefined

The crime depends on the judge

It isn't only that
the dialectical process is nonsense
(who are you going to talk to?)
What embarrasses Marxists is history.
They cannot abide the fact that
the world was interesting
without the superimposed unification
of opposites. Managers never understand
that fairness is not up to them.

Eat All You Want

Fake Fat
is the most
brilliant solution
of the 20th century.
It makes T. S. Eliot
into total protein.
It makes Dan Rather
almost correct.
It makes that morning weatherman
a genius. It makes
Joan Rivers an idiot
from the swamps.

The Claptrap Nomenklatura of Western Regimes

Zero tolerance
Will never equal Intolerance:
for that you'll need a thesis
and a hammer, and some nails
and a door!

California usage

Everyone is either
an asian or a non-asian.
There's no such thing as milk—
it's either chocolate or non-chocolate.
And life—forget that
there's death or non-death,
something Rose Bird failed
utterly to comprehend.

Stop Complaining:
On not being co-opted

If someone offers you drugs
Don't call the police—
Get out your chemistry set and test them.
Apart from avoiding super-cut
Eastern Airline product
You might save yourself the surprise
Of a bunker-like Tylenol check-out.

(note: the eagerness to avoid pain
can be deadly

Hate Without Style

If those patriots
who are sending Kadafy
their garbage in the mail
are so tough, why
don't they put it in a samsonite
and deliver it?

Philippine Phenomenology

If you can figure out
how an ecclesiastic
came by the name
Cardinal Sin
they you should be put
in charge of the national budget
of the U.S.A.

Lackey stacked upon lackey

The one red leaf, the last of its clan
sails across the crusted snow.
The afternoon is mild, water fallen weeks ago
runs in sparks under the new sun.
There's nothing to do with Valentine's day
but observe a moment of screaming
for all the love that was of no account
and all the misleading feeling.

By Definition

The construction business:
a bunch of guys
standin' around a hole
from which emanates walkie-talkie rasp
and around them hang
a semi-circle of citizens
hands cupping their ears.

An Exception for Courtroom Behavior

In Sparks, Nevada
people should be allowed
to show up drunk.

Barbed Praise

Barbed praise
is the best praise of all
in a world where
no praise is good—

as in "they touched
the face of God
because the seals broke."

Barbed Praise

People who own cats
live in a Cat House
and that might mean
savage times.

That's alright—
it's better than living
in a Dog House,
with the doggone.

An Old-Fashioned Problem: Cundurango won't help

He had gonorrhoea
of the go(ä)norhynchus
(oh, isospondyli) !

I'm Clean, how about you?

I never ordered a general
  into Central America
  although there are those who did.

I never dumped any dioxin
  at Times Beach, although
  somebody must have.

I never made any money in Lebanon,
  although I guess some people musta done.

I never put engine oil in salad dressing
  but you know it happens
  all the time in Algeria.

I never shot anybody,
  but people do it all the time
  and as far as I'm concerned,
  they're shooting the wrong people.

I've saved a few lives in my time
  just by dispensing some good advice,
  but that doesn't count
  and anyway, it's the wrong direction
  because this world cries for death
  and practically nothing else.

In that respect, I've missed
  all the big events:
I never fed any lions in the Roman Arena
I never massacred any Protestants in France
I never gassed any Jews
I never owned any Slaves

I never scalped any Indians
I never spread syphilis in Tahiti
I never macheted any joggers.

In fact, I'm an exemplary non-entity.

Why do they tell us what they tell us?

Since all the stats
are quoted as saying
Rape, Mutilation & Murder
and violent seduction
of every kind
are carried out against you, overwhelmingly,
by close friends, mere friends
and relatives,
"saying no to strangers"
should be revised
to "saying no to everyone you know."

Harvesting Organs: **On the Head-Injury Death of a 24 Year Old Boy in Vermont**

Several Specialists "flew" in from Pittsburgh.
Please pardon the anthropomorphism there.
I don't mean to suggest raptors—
they're just carrion birds.

Whereupon they tore the fucker apart,
called him Skin & Bones.
They freezedried his butt,
chilled his skin. Somebody else
is wearing it now—who *is* wearing it now?
Probably some lawyer in Topeka.
Or maybe a wag in Wichita.
The fat from his posterior
now fills out an anorexic gal in Scranton.

The heart went to Houston as usual.
There is sense in this—
Houston needs all the heart it can get.
The boy's eyes went to Denver
a place as plain as the nose on your face
in dire need of vision.

And what did Pittsburgh get?
The most perishable goods, the liver
and maybe the spleen—
whichever, you can bet Pittsburgh can use it.
Look at its history, think of its past—
it has always been a big consumer of organs.

All the other parts, right down
to the toes, all the way out to the branch banks
to someone in need of a new set of knuckles,

the boy's parts were scattered through
the vast black market of the medical abattoir,
thrifty now as the Hormel slaughterhouses
of Austin Minnesota. Yet very few, if any,
of the "recipients" would be black.

Note: the very first attempts to put
the hearts of baboons in the human breast
occurred in South Africa—the surgical anxiety
to find a primate substitute
for the scandal of the obvious.

Ah well, even as we repose here
studying the ramifications
of this cryogenic express,
they're out there, under the flashy lights,
gleaning the fallen fruit, the strange fruit—
and this time it's the bourgeoisie who are gathered.
After all, they run around the most,
they are the fittest.

Ode on the Facelifting of the "statue" of Liberty

America is inconceivable without drugs
and always has been. One of the first acts
was to dump the tea. The drug that furnished
the mansions of Virginia was tobacco,
a drug now in much disrepute.
Sassafras, a cure-all, is what they came for
and they dealt it by the bale altho it
was only a diaphoretic to make you perspire —
people were so simple in those days.
The Civil War saw the isolation of morphine
making amputation a pleasure and making
the block of wood between the teeth,
which was no drug, obsolete. Morphinism
was soon widespread among doctors *and* patients.
At this date interns, the reports tell us,
are among the premier drug ab/users
of said moralistic nation. "Rock" stars
(who notoriously "have" doctors)
consume drugs by the metric ton
even as they urge teenagers to Say No.
The undercurrent of American history
has been the running aches and pains
of the worn path to the door of the apothecary
to fetch cannabis and cocaine elixirs
by the gallon. It has been all prone
all seeking Florida, Ponce de León
was just the beginning of a statistical curve
whose only satisfaction would be total vertigo.
His eager search for youth has become our
frantic tilt with death and boredom,
in fact we are farming death in Florida
with far greater profit than we are
farming food in Iowa—elixirs are as multiform

as the life-style frauds we implore,
a cultural patchwork fit for a fool
in the only country in the world
with a shop called the Drug Store.

Aincha sick of 'em?

The U.S. turned thumbs down
on a Soviet offer to release
Nicholas Daniloff today.
Guess they didn't want him back.

It's still their entrapment
against ours.
Maybe they should
hire Pat Robertson
to just *suck* 'im back,
with the power of The Lord

Or do they use that
term anymore?
My ears tell me
the euphemism God
has supplanted the Lord.

Well, whatever it is,
it sure could be lordosis
which produces a convexity
in front.

18 September, 1986
A soup of liberals
in which float chunks
of high protein praetors.

Welcome Home

Riding across the arid plains
through scattered entrenchments of plywood
we come from the Denver Aerodrome
to the small, consumerist
space station of Balderdash.
It advertises the fact that it is
the sister-city of some wretched
little town in Central America,
to which it sends blankets, cans of food,
and an occasional party of sympathizers,
led by a creaking mayor
who is barely able to gush anymore,
but in whom there are several goshes left.

Yea, though I am scarcely able myself
to surrejoin their measly works
my indifference runneth over,
waiting for the light to change
at Broadway and Cañon
next to a smoking Cherokee,
in front of a halting Mustang,
adjacent to a dented Apache, facing,
across the intersection,
a preposterous Winnebago.

Jar Wars II

Just saying no to drugs
is an idea whose time
passed long ago.

Saying no to tylenol
would have been a stroke of genius
for several users,

but for a lot of users
Bye Bye to Thalidomide
would have saved some Koochi-Koo
for the babies with flippers
and five eyes.

A B H O R R E N C E S
29 September, 1986
Low tech or no tech,
say pleez or no cheez—
by the goofs of techniki.

Proprietary Rights and Patented Germs

The bacillus slaves,
trucked in by the truckload.
Some thicken toothpaste,
some ripen cheeze, Cheddar.
Some churn butter.
Some turn the blades of helicops,
others create smiles on thy face.
Others make thy cars, including
the upholstery—those be
Cadillac enzymes. All the glitches
and runts of that breed are Hondas.
Another strain produce thy Fundamentalists.
The Moon manifists and hitches
Ten Million People Who Don't
Even Know Each Other!
There's a germ for that.

There's literally no end to it,
to what they can do.
The proprietary virus
is throughout thy body—
Bio-Catalysm is the way to go.
Buy into it, it's thy only hope.
Thy money will percolate
right into thy foot,
no more worries, no more waiting for thy boat.
No more dreadin' o' the Tijuana steroids
because they put screw-worms in thy kidney.
With this yeast thou can spray on
a swatch of Schwartzenegger and watch the cules pop.

And maybe in thy more perfect future
thou'll spray on sex organs, and the clothes
to go with them—Presto! transexual surgeons
out of work. Surely, the most spectacular enzymes
will always remain the most secret of secret things.
Meanwhile, back in the Icey 90ies,
it was easier to make a hole than a pole.

Cyndi Lauper

"We didn't really
realize what was
going on in Europe
until we went to Japan
and Australia"

Entropy

No matter how smart
an individual may be
they're going to look
not so smart on t v.

Radio Nostalgia

Yes, we put a man
on the moon and

We should have left
the son-of-a-bitch there.

18 October 1986
incest is best
liverwurst is worst

Every example tells a story

Like everything else
rock & roll
is here to go away.

On Losing One's Coolant

Along about the 6th inning
of game 7, intense loathing
for the Mets and things "New York"
spilled out of me like
dark, apoplectic lava
whereupon I stuck a few pins
in my Ed Koch doll.

America the Buick

A smouldering red light—
in front of me a Buick
with only the U I remaining
on its cracked white paint job.
The roof lining hangs
with tattered effrontery
and could harbor bats.
Coils of patched flex
bounce and twist in the backseat
like hollow pythons who have adapted
to a diet of carbon monoxide.

It all creeps off then
to yet another useless, low-scandal,
shady, local destination.
It's not a compact, it's not a mid-size.
It's stretched alright,
but the work
wasn't done in a body shop.

Condom mania: the ins and outs

Latex tappers in Liberia
are taking home the pay
like oil drillers used to do in Texas
before the price-fixing fell apart
under creeping greed and holy wars.

As anyone who has ever tried
to use a "condom" knows
they're rubbery and freaky
and only utter perverts would
entertain even the idea.

Besides that, they are known
to be full of holes
punched in by bored and dissatisfied
workers in the same spirit
and with the same motives
as certain HIV carriers, whose
industrial revenge is not saying no
but passing it on—

Or that workers in canning factories
hock gobs of sputum into beans, corn,
okra, hash, spam, Chung Foo,
soy boo, Chef Boyardee
& black-eyed pea.

But forget all that,
who the hell ever
called'em condoms anyway.

Hi Hype Budgette

When you spend more
on defending the thing
than you spend
on the thing you're defending.

The Public Service Message

It is reiterated:
the charge will fall
most heavily on
the old & the poor.
A lot of the poor are young
but all of the old are old.
This is the style of new justice
to pre-select longevity.

Gargling Draino

Note: Jenny—Rec'd phone call
while at the mailboxes
from the assistant to the guy
you'll have to bill. Somewhere
out there, there's some horrible bastard
of either sex with nothing to do
but order a single copy.

Hazardous Sex (as distinct from "safe sex")

Sex with an electronic bug.
Sex with a pig routed for the sausage machine in the Hormel
plant
Sex with a peach farmer during an early spring blizzard.
Sex with the police in Santiago during the Pope's visit, likewise
sex with the Pope.
Gangsex with a group of Libyans carrying machine guns &
money.
Sex with a person who is being deported by the INS for being an
Arab.
Sex of any kind with an executive like Waka Ohji in Tokyo.
Sex with anyone being subjected to an electrical charge.
Quick sex with individuals on temporary visas.
Sex with a lame duck is out of the question.
And obviously, and no matter how tempting, sex with Soviet
women.

A B H O R R E N C E S
Somewhere in the Eighties
The death of pop

A Circus of Hokum
or how many cookie jars make a bushel

A string of Little Boys
(funding the Rebels)
Congressional bleeding
(o noh noh miss cho)
last minute legislation
(continuing resolution)
lengthy in-house reviews
(the underlying cause)
In the end, was he
actually killed by the bible?
(the nurse, after all,
was reading the bible).

historical cure-all
(rockets not rocks

A Coup de Guerre in a Teacup

What the Palestinians
need to do is
bring back the Philistines.

"An unrecorded act is not one that never took place"

It isn't that the Ollie & Fawn follies
are without entertainment
but that the poverty of vocabulary
surrounding them is so severe.

Why not give them a little credit
by describing their attitude
for what it is, namely Fuckoffistic.
This quality was never more evident
than when Fawn spoke her now quasi-famous
passage regarding the need, sometimes,
to be Above the Law, thus arousing
such incredulous indignation
although one wonders why since
she could have as appropriately said
"below the law."

A time to buy and a time to cry

These are the official symptoms
of cocaine use:
weight loss, insomnia,
nausea, anxiety,
radical alcohol
and tobacco intake,
chronic irritation,
helpless involuntary verbalism,
possibly leading
to fulminant dementia —

Wait a minute!
except for weight loss,
those are just the pathologies
of an afternoon
spent at the shopping mall.

Hand Held Refrigerator

Every time he crushed
his styrofoam cup
he blew a hole in the ozone cover.

Idle thoughts at the St Marks
20th anniversary reunion

Ed Sanders is the only optimist
the Greeks ever produced

Allen Ginsberg is the only poet
the Greeks never produced

The Differently Abled

The Eighties inventiveness
in pseudo-categories
probably reached its apex
when it was announced
that this guy in Oklahoma
could crack nuts
using his dick as a hammer.

The momentum of the excrementum

The late Eighties really got frantic:
Oral Roberts claim to have raised the dead
pushed John Lennon's boast about being
bigger than Christ through the roof,
and some Georgia jerk's claptrap about
running a car on who knows what
but probably frijoles. Ah,
the steaks were high,
and the sperm was great.

Off the Waldheim

The Papal Audience is about as low as it gets
So Waldheim has still got a long way to climb
He looks like what in the Midwest
They used to call a "cheap son-of-a-bitch"
But I don't mind him because there's only
One level now, even though there are distinctions
Herr Waldheim equals about sixty Chrysler Execs
With disconnected odometers, but his real offense
was cozying up to the Palestinians at the U.N.

A B H O R R E N C E S
Summer 1987
Linoleum Tattoos

Some Things Do Change

Now they build the house
around the swimming pool
In the Middle Ages
they built the swimming pool
around the house.
The Middle Ages were a lot smarter—
they built swimming pools for their enemies.

The Independent Boulder Woman

The Independent Boulder Woman
is somewhere between forty & fifty
and looks precisely 38 and a few months.

The IBW is not so much divorced
as unhooked.
S/he goes out with younger men
and speaks of them
as a good or bad lay
much as a guy might speak of a girl.

The IBW drives a late model Japanese car
usually, but not a few
affect the Germans and the Scandinavians.

An "I love my Volvo" bumpersticker
on the other hand, signals
an almost certain confusion
in the sub-species.

Italian cars are not popular
among Boulder's IW,
and one never sees a Russian car
in Boulder at all—
although one could hypostatize
that driving a Russian car
in Colorado would be the mark
of arch independence.

When the IBW sees
a parking meter
with an "official use only"
hood on it,

she pulls right in—
she knows it's bullshit,
and besides,
who could be more
official than her?

At a 4-way stop sign the IBW
will *rarely* wait her turn.
To do so would be self-denying
and anyway, those other three drivers
can't possibly have any place
so urgent to get to.

Altho the IBW disdains
the Book of Genesis,
she will not attack Judeo-
Christian business directly
for to do so might deny
a nun somewhere who prays
to be president.

The IBW often double
as land jobbers (real estate agents
to those with no fund of history)
having acquired their stake
through a settlement,
in which fortuitous circumstance
they are Landlords as well.
But IBW are notably capitalistic
in many ways. They are prominent
in the "Small Business Community":
fancy, if not fantastic, lingerie shops,
so-called health and image promoting
schemes of all stamps, the whole
dress for success spectra.

The IBW, whatever else
she knows about Nicaragua,
probably approves of Daniel Ortega's
Three Thousand Dollars worth

of designer specs, the purchase of which,
on a United Nations visit, so
annoyed our President.

Everywhere the IBW goes,
she knows, men are a joke,
possibly, even, a fluke.

Our Independent Boulder Woman
may or may not smoke, and
it may or may not be advised
to test her urine,
but in either case, to her,
it will be "no joke."

IBW toenote

The IBW is notorious
for running red lights —
sometimes she's broadsided
right in the middle of the section
but what the hell
hanging around
for the light to change
is not really driving anyway.

Cooking the Corpse

And yet again, another
chance at coinage
has been missed
by failing to label
Casey's fortuitous kick-off,
for the witnesses,
a necro-opportunity—
and furthermore, this
in a time when Opportunity
has been the guiding principle
in politics, economy & disease.

Would You Repeat the Question

Let's forget the awesome moral goofyness
suggested by the term Deniability
and consider the far profounder
implications of "I don't recall
or I don't Think I recall,
whether I put it in the Out
or in the In basket."

Martyrs Opera

It's all way behind California here—
not much satanism to speak of,
the big sacrifices are to Impatience
and the sufferance of the routinely insufferable:
a too long queque into Full Metal Jaquette,
too few Xtians with too small bullhorns
at the opening of the celluloid
temptation of the Lord
almost reconverts the neo-nonsmokers.
But they don't need it—the smoke
still smoulders in their overcooked brains,
and melts the aloe on their malevolent lips.

Gaudy, laminated portraits of themselves
hang from their necks
not the image of some fearsome mullah,
not even close—they have so little neck
and no stiff devotion. When they break
their coffee grinders
they blow off their retarded dogs
with lawn darts assembled in Ciudad Juarez,
and do not think twice.
But that's good—the fact that
they think once is the horror of it.

Vizutek

That's where
you just see
whatcha wanta

Credo Alfredo

I will never shop
at Banana Republic.
Never. Ever.

But I will go down
to Banana Republic
and I will take hostages
among the customers, only
the fat ones perhaps,
but no! The thin ones—
there are more of them.
And I'll ship off
the whole lot with only their belts
to chilly North Dakota. Where
there are bananas all right,
whole counties full.

All in the name of child-proof caps

It isn't that time flies,
it doesn't, it pokes along
looking for a handicapped space
which is always empty
and always illegal. Like
most normal people, whose hearts
are not made of copper,
I have a certain sympathy
for Nixon, one of the first
of the homeless. He had
trouble lining up the markers
on medicine bottles. It's
quite likely the whole Gate suffix
and the demagogic inflation
of the record
was just the result of the misalignment
of the markers on the mood elevators.

A Dispatch from the Front

The campaign by the City of Boulder
(the cutest little town in the west)
now current, to levy a tax
on the hides of the pedestrians
must be one of the queerest actions
in these so-called states.

The Motor Vehicle & Bicycle Lobbies,
when they aren't screaming at each other,
are notoriously powerful & together here,
mainly because car owners and bicyclists
practically cohabit, in the land of
the big bicycle rack.

It's true, pedestrians really do
slow things up—and this is a town
that hates to wait more than Anything.

Two, four or for that matter six legs
don't make any difference here.
If you're a man (white-guy, one might
as well be honest—there are few others
in the venue)
they'll nail your hide to the asphalt.

If you're a dog shivering
in the chilly Boulder night
trying to exit the graveyard
having peed on Tom Horn's headstone
or howling at the mouth of the canyon
they'll nail your hide to the asphalt.

If you're a cat, sick on Science Diet,
headed for the other side of the concrete,
in hot pursuit of some cat meat
they'll nail your scrawny ass to the asphalt.

If you're a squirrel (frankly, I'd like
to see more squirrels end up in flatland)
with a nut in your cheeks, headed
for the great nut roundup,
they'll chase you right up the tree.

If you're a spider, trying to take
advantage of the sun, or merely
the lack of rain, a bicycle wheel
as big as a train will crush you,
and all your spider parts
will be printed, vaguely, on the asphalt.

You will be doomed even more than a man
because you are older, and have eight legs.

But the deeper problem with pedestrians
is, they fall into two categories
which can appear very similar at times:
Those actually on foot,
and those who are merely *in transit*
from a parking space to some other place.

Now, no one wants to run down the latter
in order to eliminate the former—
after all, it could be your mother
(although in this town it might not matter).

At ten bucks a crack, the charge for J-walking,
the income is probably small change so far—
although it all adds up. But as the war goes on,
and times get hard as they are bound to,
and as walkers increase, so will the revenues.

And then the fixing habit is inevitable—
they say this of drugs, they say it
of embezzlement. Why should this be any different?
Eventually bicyclists will be deputized
to arrest walkers when they get in the way
and when this proves not enough,

They will be authorized to hit them.
And that will create a usage we don't
now have: *Sidewalk Kill.* And then,
some clever thinker will publish
a book of photographs of pedestrian
hide patterns, so that you may identify,

Not only the species, but for the human hides
the origin: Southern European, South
of the Border, West of the Pecos, mixed randomly
with the occasional hapless non-ethnic
probably trying to exit, trembling with fear,
the Ideal Market complex.

One of the strongest signs that this is all so
and not the raving of a sensitive observer
is the new bicycle freeway the university
has caused to be laid along Broadway
across the main artery of foot traffic
into and out of the institution: you could
drive a Kenworth Diesel on the space for bicycles,
whereas the measly strip for walkers
will barely accommodate a baby carriage.

The Hatch Catch

What's a few rads to Hatch
whose jaws are of sculpted lanolin
with a tongue of pure latex
and lips of beeswax
from the state insect
and hydraulic skillets
serving for ears, off which
bounce the downwind bleats
of the chernobylized
Utah sheep shaggers.
Is there no fate then
too hard
for the people of the wooden submarine.

the hazards of a later era:
variation on a theme

I would like to thank you
for the plums that were
in the ice-box, but
I'm afraid I just can't
do it—in the first place
it's not an ice-box, and the plums
having come from California
are a mix of over-ripe
and hard-as-rocks,
both undesirable states,
no doubt shot through
with systemic chemicals.
Add to all that
the fact that I put
them there myself
and you have
the whole sorry picture.

Silver's Up a Nickel

Far in the past,
years ago, when I was much younger
and when the fires by which I nightly burned
had colossal fuel but still more hunger
and the subject people were far younger
                              and more spurned,
it was nothing, a morning's work
                    in a pitiable poet's life.
To have as little then was more
                              than anyone deserved.
Then our little would be spread
                    across the common strife,
and no one thought the less the more they served.
But now the coals are heaped around our guts—
throw them out, bring them in, turn
                              them into us—
we have the petulant dreams
they have the provident buts
they have it all, all but the impetus.

Heart of Copper

The Candidate, answering a question
about El Salvador, generalized
by saying he thought
we should support human rights
everywhere they were being abrogated—
South Korea, South Africa
or South Yemen. He didn't have
the moral perspicuity
to mention South Dakota.
Perhaps it's too far north.

So Long Pardner, you're bound to be better than 1988

When the world had a C word
(you can read anything for that you want)
the P word (likewise) was affective
(and you don't have to read anything
for that)
But now that it doesn't
it's pretty resentful
insofar as it can even muster it
of anything remotely
and what isn't
construed (not that you can do that)

Nineteen Eighty Eight Maniac

I'm going to take this fucking year
For which I've been waiting a long time
And I am going to rip it from its sappy
Stupid throat to its overfermented balls
And then I'm going to wrap its toxic guts
Around the first sports announcer I hear.

Life is a Lake of lukewarm pinkish yellow snot

There was the time we wasted
on the funny forelock of Hodding Carter
the Georgia Christian's guy
who had to deal with the viperish rhetoric
flowing from the mouth of the Ayatolla.
Then, after the people had expressed
their preference and the elected
had run through several others,
some worn out, shot or exposed
ruddy faced Marlin was thrust upon us,
skin mold gone public, a real fugitive
from a North Dakota Moose herd.

A question seldom asked and never answered

How often should men
who have had sex-change surgery
have pap smears?
Once a year? more frequently?
every three years?
How can we get this word
out to such males?
Where do they live,
where do they work?
what are their box numbers?

Permission Refused

I used to say Frisco all the time —
but now that it's OK I'll stop.

Recollections of Advice to Whiteguys

Be observant of people around you;
Anyone could be a terrorist.

Avoid piles of luggage or unattended bags.
If you hear gunfire,
Which sounds like catspit,
Or an explosion, fall flat on the ground
But remember, if you do this involuntarily,
You're already dead and everything
you see is just a re-run.

Never sit near windows
or any kind of glass, never go near glass.
Always sit with your back to windows,
Things have changed a lot
Since Bill Hickok's day.

Never let a bellhop take your bags,
Do anything, a karate chop, a sharp
kick in the groin—but even better,
Never have any bags. And never
Attend unscheduled meetings,
But to any meeting always take along
An armed witness.

Be observant, but don't overreact.
In most cases you will be ignored
Or worse, charged. If you have bad feelings
About anyone around you, leave immediately
But not with alarm—don't look back
Let your witness do that.

Especially be wary of "friendly locals,"
the original terrorists. Look around,
Evaluate. Who is weak, who, in biting,
Has swallowed the bullet?
Nervous wrecks should definitely be avoided.

Finally, avoid heated discussions.
Don't panic. Be cooperative.
Never make gratuitous sudden movements.
Eschew stickers like "Up the Army" or
"I Love New York." Hit the Deck. Leave Quickly.
Above all, don't be proud—
In the event of fire you may have
To crawl through heavy smoke.

Neolojizem

"Unacceptable"
is a strange term
used by the
politically impotent
to describe whatever's
being shoved down
their collective throat.

"Handle me lustily . . . ere the blood-rush cease"

Nay, not for the Prophet will I plunge my toe therein!
For the banks of curious Maximus are parcelled into sites,
Commanded and embellished and patrolled by Olsonites.

The thing's too heavy, should have been put on
fine bible paper to give it wave, which is inherent
all the way through its vast Counter Reformation systemics.

And the inking isn't perfect, it's got California
stiff-as-a-board sensibility all over it.
The dark, threatening, diamond studded
baton of the neo cortex leeches out into the Nowhere.
It smells like eucalyptus instead of cod.

But I'm concerned, everybody around here's concerned.
Therefore we pass it around the table
and for some time thereafter
we throw words all over the page.

■

"Where there is wealth
let us create excess . . .
where there is need,
let us create hardship,
where there is poverty,
let us create downright misery."

Quatrain Naboko

I kicked a wasp
out of my cabin,
told it to come back
when it was a butterfly.

Hi Stix Jungle—
A town dreaming of
machine guns—
Spitting rounds,
but snoring &
jerking
July 17th '88

Motel Superbo

A sleepwalker from Continent I
prints out the contract
and hands me a key attached
to a leg iron.
The drapes, heavy with fire retarder,
won't quite shut. The air condish
is clogged with breath of dead carpet.
Kim Basinger is crazy for sex
on HBO, gimme mo say Steamboat Springs.
Dodge Rams charge and butt
along the main drag.
The blasé traffic lights control
with cold indifference the snarling,
big pipe packs, sends them along
and then pins them to the tar
where they whine and gnash
at the electronic tether,
sending tics through the ignorant sleepers.

Progress: slow but inexorable

He set out to buy the American Dream.
First, he went to a yard sale
and bought himself a yard.
Then, he went to a garage sale
and bought a garage.
Next, he went to a porch sale
and bought a big porch.
Now all he needed was a swing
and a house and a car.

Population Control in Boulder

Bright zebras mark the free zone,
freshly painted foot-traps.
A chocolate man in a chocolate van
leans forward, looks left and turns right
over a pair of careful old ladies
crossing their very last street.
One of them is squashed like a tick
and immediately heads west,
the other is rushed to emergency
where she becomes a lucrative customer
in a coma—but not for long—
three days later they pull the curtains
and close the books.

There follows some public discussion
and a fair amount of low-grade,
Reagan Era indignation, but everybody knows
pediforms are on their own in Bo-town.

ABHORRENCES
22 August, 1988
Rangoon
"We deplore the
the shooting of
unarmed demonstrators.

Stupid as a One way street

I like Phyllis Oakley—she's
overweight, she's sad and patient,
she's resentful that she can't
eat candy while stating the position
she doesn't enjoy being looked at
and her habit being judged
anymore than a demonstrator
likes being shot. She's a far way
better presenter than Redman
the terrified twit.
Throughout the troubles
we've had the most medically odd
apologists—why is that?

Solo Pretendre

The Persians have been at it
for three millennia,
the present horde of Californians
for eight years—though some of them
arrived in town yesterday
and haven't even unpacked their "bags."
With the summer's examination of Poindexter
one has to concur once again
with the Ayatollah—was there ever
a greater shortage of dexter?

But the mullahs are obviously
not connoisseurs of Satans.
They should stop using the word great.
They should read Milton.

ABHORRENCES
Summer, 1988,
when Ralph Nader
was in town

Oecological Caution

I drive everywhere.
It's not that I'm against walking
But I don't like the look
of the pedestrians.

A Summer Evening in Boulder

A table full of plastic and bottlecaps
which leave a ringworm of themselves behind,
jugs with foreign labels and strong alcohol
in all its arabic fluency and sin,
a crowd of the not so young but rather young,
a ninety-five-thousand dollar house,
too short for a tall man but just right for most
and worth about 58 if true value were merely a fraud.
For the audio some late, high amp Led Zep, which
when you heard it in 1971 was a welcome scream
but now sounds like a corpse
dying of AIDS in the trunk of a hairdresser's plymouth.
A climactic smell, as if
a vast candidatorial factory, promising work
to millions of persons who will produce excrement
wafts through the screen, through the casement,
across the spit-turned suslik and chicken wings.
The struggle is true and not new—
the poor things have People magazine
to thank for everything, and yet
they could have done the boogaloo like so many of us—
a badly timed generation really, particularly unfortunate
and in the grip of forces determined to make them renters.
This is the Eighties coming to a close.
This is the edge of the smokeless plain
where the plutonium blows
and the buffalo moan.

ABHORRENCES
15 Sept. '88
take it easy
on the organs

Blunt Force Trauma

The windblown scream of the siren
is the final municipal salute
to the memory of a dead ped
crushed & waiting to be carried away
by the dachshunds of small business
who will sort the parts. Everyone benefits.
The killer's insurance is now schluckened
and the premiums hit the top,
the luder's case will be put out to bid
in some other state, probably California
where they live on the corpses
of the whole west and blow the profits
on more whips and chains. The carting service
will tender its bill, and the bill will be heavy.
The police and the toilers at the law
will levy their levy
and they will be way heavy.
If drinks have been drunk, the mothers
will be madder, if dope is discovered
in the trunk property will be seized,
new cells built and taxes laid on.
It's an apparently perfect machine —
who says perpetual motion is unattainable.

ABHORRENCES
30 September, '88
Thanks a lot
for the ticket to die

Don't just stand there, get something!

But the worship of Liberty
(always shielded
by the vile euphemism Freedom—
a usage appropriate only to birds
and other wingéd things)
became so demented in the mid-Eighties
that it took on the defense of running sores
and plagues, and pustules
and the whole torture of Job
which nobody ever had to suffer
except Job and several thousand Argentines.

It was all evanescence
but don't cut yourself, and don't read
Masters & Johnson's chapter on how
condoms are like putting a white glove
on your hand and sticking it in the mouth of a crocodile.

Lock the Door

I'm goin' down
to the church
to pray

Gonna get
down on
my knees
and stay

ABHORRENCES
30 Oct, '88
the war between
the clinics &
the lunatics
& the drug makers

Thou Shalt Not Kill:
Oh Yes I Will!

They beat each other on the haid
with foetuses by Rubber Maid
Some dump anti-ulcer medicine
which is said to abort the problem
Others work at devices
which cause pro-lifers to get pregnant
so's they'll have to live with it
They all really hate each other like scat
If they'd just annihilate each other
we could leave it at that

Holy Weenies

The mall is crawling.
They're trying to change
the name to Boo
but it will always crawl.

Space persons by the thousand
from the salmonella chicken factory of Longmont
and the plutonium nets of Broomfield
are milling with a little alcohol
and a lota seconal in their tummies.
The sky is overcast,
air Jordans are on their hairy feet.

Stupid grins are on their mugs,
Registered Idiots on their handles.
It's a fearsome, contagious crowd.
They don't know AIDS from a bedbug.
Whoa-oa! this is deep creep actino—
trepidation without frills, Praise the Lord!
I'm getting it on radio.

Smoke that Cigarette

It's quite ironic, come to think of it
that the contra-smokers waited
a quarter of a millennium
to lodge their objections—smoke stacks
never seemed to bother them, in fact
smoke stacks still don't. Maybe its because
from those far huger symbols
they get their electricity.
Bless them, they are such earnest hypocrites.

The re-PUBlicans!!!

Meat on the table. Women dancing
Las Vegas Nordic style. Mock chickens
artfully carved from raw beef
complete with wriggling worms
in their well carved beaks.
Little jap cars dripping with oel
stacked in the garage
where once was a simple,
broadbacked Cadillac. From the spit
the smell of roasting Losers.

The sound of ten-thousand throats
raised in song. The rich
taste of Victory in every mouth.
rePUBlicans!
Chief George the Supercilious
quaffed a horn of Houstonian proportions
and punched a Greek in the head
and swaggered to his feet,
a huge oath on his lips
which could be read from the farthest reaches
of the vast Hall—
"WENCHE!!! A horn of QualeAle
for the rePUBlican WarLord!"

Suddenly, from amongst the Midwestern Horde
a cheque-clad warrior lurched to his knees.
"Raiders!" he cried,
his short blonde hair sprayed to his head,
"I be Chief Danforth the Indianan—
I come from the Great Polluted Wabash Estate.
Raise with me and my freckled clan

159

your horns in honor of our leader
in battle this day, the Great War Chieftain
George the Super Official,
who has laid on the red chicken
and gravy and QualeAle."

The mighty, blood-spattered rePUBlicans
roared and punched each other till
they were Red and White and Blue.

George the Supercilious threw back his head
and howled: "Today we have won
a neet Victory for the MultiLords—
we have Lynched the Libs, Mauled the Massites,
Buggered the Pinks and Wanked
the Wage Slaves,
we have repo'd their wretched hovels!!!"

Just then Edd the Meachum from the Dry Zone,
from the Water Thieves Estate, walked in
and said, casually, "Guess what
I've just Found?"

"WHAT?!!!" roared the Maddened Pachyderms.

"Mexico."

"CHIHUAHUA!!!" bayed the lagered Rogues,
their horns aloft, sloshing over with Korona.

ABHORRENCES
General Eighties
the Homeless,
what Veblen wld
have instantly recognized
as invidious in the old
style, or my right
to be excluded has become
the profit of your guilt.

**The result
of a society composed of castaways**

The signature of the flow of money,
the unlimited authority to issue visas
to the quaking swarms of sick and maimed.
The solution for new york would now seem
to be to tax the homeless for being homeless,
a Grate Rate, or Toilet to Let.

The problem is—what to charge 'em.
For much of the recent past they gave their blood,
but that is now corrupted with all the blood supply.
One thinks in an updated way Dog Feed—
the trend is definitely to dogs. The breakup
of the family (and again, Veblen would appreciate this)
produced dogs on a scale to merit a census.
Dogs should be trained to vote. A dog should
be president—A REAL Dog that is. And it should
be against the law for people to shit on the street.

The Degeneration of the Greeks

It was said—timeo Danaos
et dona Ferentes. "I fear the Greeks
even when they bring gifts."
That was a long time ago. Still,
it should have meant something
at the end of a weak decade like the 80^{ies}.
It meant something to me,
and so I voted. I didn't care
that Kitty had a speed problem,
that only made me more hopeful,
a first Lady who talked like an A head,
I thought, would be a relief.
But thousands upon thousands
of idiot savants didn't agree with me.
They apparently wanted to hear the high pitched
bicarbonate ignorance of mere oil wells.
Texas has a lot on its head—it's
costing us too much, it isn't carrying
its weight in ideas, it should be
returned to Mexico, it should have offal
in its streets, it should have cops
who ride on motorscooters and make their lives
a misery of bribes, and their beef should
hang in the open market covered with flies.

ABHORRENCES
15 May 1989
It isn't what you get
it's what you take.

Euphemismo Inc.

Did anybody need a neologism
for revisionism, or at least
doesn't it seem a little early?

New Age is well nigh perfect —
tired and toothless,
tried and truthless . . . one
hundred and eighteen gears,
all of those indistinguishable,
which means that if they were on fire
you couldn't put it out
because the flame is so low
it burns not. It just burns without hot,
it's better than fusion in a pot.

A B H O R R E N C E S
a little solace
for the Turin Shroud
Tee Shirt Brigade
10 March, 1989

Don't give up, it's only natural

The envy all writers felt like a needle
when Rushdie got his sentence,
far greater award than the dynamite prize,
is almost impossible to convey.
Even Norman Mailer, the literary Napoleon
was moved to follow instead of lead.
Such flights of fancy, such fame and fortune.
Such mock and useless blasphemy,
such testimony to the desperation
visited upon this trade
by a wholly indifferent Judeo-Christo clink of coin
where the wrack has grown cobwebs
and the boiling oil has long cooled.
Tolerance has ruined us all
like hopping frogs with nowhere to hop.
If what you say isn't worth your life
then you're just wasting time
like everybody else, and for a writer
that's an even more awful truth.

ABHORRENCES
Sam's Bar & Mosque
Downtown Alliance, Neb.,
March, 1989

Rushdie Bumper Sticker

HIT ME!

ABHORRENCES
23 March, 1989
We're going to have
to do better than this.

Mediocre Friday

In Rome the Pontiff carried a crucifix,
not a very big one though.
In Valdees the tanker carried
a cargo of crude,
but not for very long.
In Australia I suppose they said
G'die as usual,
but that didn't change anything —
it was still a mediocre Friday.

A B H O R R E N C E S
Lite Gulag,
the poverty industry
takes off — 24 April, '89

The Sin Casas

Capitalism in action
Open prisons in the street
The creatures of the vents
& cardboard coffins
Packing-case sarcophagi
Not awfully permanent
But better than the poison sky
The pool of the puking
Lorded over by the AIDS barons
Moved on by the Keepers of the Tedium
The props who are supposed
To make the minions cringe.

A B H O R R E N C E S
Half-witted Factotem,
date uncertain, but
probably around the
end of May, a particulary
stupid month in 1989.

Jim Wright

Polish luxury brought him down
and Latin heresy saw him off.
Which is fine, old time corruption
is always preferable to new grease.
It's a smug victory, full of almost
exquisitely boring detail.
There was the occasion when
he went to that Central American Country—
What could they have thought of his hair,
parted in the middle, and those dreadful,
opticians eyeglasses. A voice,
there's no getting around it,
which says, Even though you think I'm lying,
I'm going to make your palm a gusher
of lubricant, it shall be like
a dream of dividends—we are about to send off
a man who took the american dream
and drove it to the station. Scratch me
and you'll make a million. Why else come here?
Ask any injun, that's the first thing they noticed.

A B H O R R E N C E S
Gimme a break on
Korruption, it has
replaced Apple Pie.
31 May, 1989

When Values Get Relative, Value Gets Going

The worse John Power was,
the better he got, sawed-off,
virile little fucker, everything
"america" admires, everything it wants,
and everything the rest of the world
sends us, and everything said
hemisphere deserves, he exemplified.
I, personally, aside from my better Judgement,
didn't object to him that much. Of
the Rip-offs on the menu he was
at least trying to make an honest buck
out of Arms & Munitions—at least
that's traditional, since we don't
manufacture anything else now—and it Is
a fair market, the appliances of death
must be the same as stupid chips
everybody seems to think they need
to replace their so-called brains
now disguised as blue to cover the green.
Drunks, secret smokers, Paper Robber Barons,
importers of cheap labor, scratchy moralists
ready to bid on the removal of the wall—
isn't that it—the bid on hauling away the wall.
If those other Germans have any sense at all
they'll keep that wall, and defend it to the death.

ABHORRENCES
In the smoke of
the "Western" media glee
over the spilt blood
laced with a little ap-
prehension for reduced
business. 7 June, 1989

Free Market Chinoiserie

There will never be enough BMWs
for the stated Billion, there will never
even be enough paper towel
or gas barbecues or ever enough ribs
or sauce for those short ribs. There will never
be enough coupons to clip or scissors
to clip them with—and there will never be
enough accountants to count it all
or paper to keep the accounts on
or discs to store the accounts
for which there will never be entries enough.
Someone should tell them.

Come to SOUTH AMERICA
a Continental Theme Park

SEE
Fascism in Action
Authentic Dictators
Victims of Torture with fresh cigarette burns
Observe the clash of Ideologies
between Rightwing and Leftwing Clergy
Witness the masses starving in front of your eyes.

See Cocaine Lords spraying lead on judges,
on Rivals, on Coffee Barons, on stray cats
and mangy dogs along palm-lined avenues.

SEE
Right-wing Novelists run for the Presidency of Peru
and get elected and then assassinated
by the Sendero Luminoso

SEE
cia Helicopters spray coca bushes with Feed & Weed
in Bolivia and cheer when they are blown out of the sky
by rockets made in CHINA!

TAKE RIVER TRIPS
See the last tree in the last rainforest dehydrated
by the killer of the Treaty Oak, flown in for the occasion

All accommodations guaranteed sanitized, pure water,
mosquito free environment, or free mosquitoes where
desired—no liability assumed for the Noriega Bullwhip
bugger sessions in Panama. Book early. Don't miss this
rapidly degenerating venue.

171

ABHORRENCES
Wherein the Rushees
mean to get good & rushed.
Some late afternoon
anthropoetry among
the Golden Boughs
beyond my french doors.
Very early September, '89,
a year that will live in
infamy, if it lives at all.

Routines, Immane proceedings, Handclaps

The Kewt gestapo girls of Tri Delta
are hoppin' and stompin' & boostin' and grindin'
in their shaded flagstone courtyard.
their yells are pseudo-tribal
and if the stats are to be trusted,
their hopechests are neo-bridal.
The audience? The recruits
are as still as mice with an extra gene,
transfixed in the glare of a robocat.

ABHORRENCES
Forget the bullwhips,
the voodoo mammy, the
agent who hung the
picture of Adolph (art
deco dictator) in the closet—
pick up St. George's securifone . . .

Panama:

An embarrassingly public dogfight
Between two official dope dealers
Closes the book on a churlish decade
Right in the very shadow of the Millennium—
All of it reported without any weight
By the scurrying insects of neologism
To a barefoot and pregnant enclave
North of the Rio Grande.

The End

Did you know that
when they execute you in China
they send your next of kin
a bill for 1 Yang (28¢)
to cover the cost of the bullet?
This is the very definition
of frugal management.
Maybe Bush can learn something
from Deng after all, maybe
there's a pow-wow under the kow-tow.

It's a good thing Reagan
didn't know about this practise.
He'd have considered it tax relief.

Printed May 1990 in Santa Barbara & Ann
Arbor for the Black Sparrow Press by Graham
Mackintosh & Edwards Brothers Inc. Text set in
Trump by Words Worth. Design by Barbara Martin.
This edition is published in paper wrappers;
there are 300 hardcover trade copies;
150 hardcover copies have been numbered & signed
by the author; & 26 copies handbound in boards
by Earle Gray are lettered & signed by the author.

Photo: Chris Felver

Edward Dorn was born in 1929 and grew up in Eastern Illinois, on the banks of the river Embarrass (a tributary of the Wabash). He never knew his father. His mother was of French ancestry, his grandfather a railroad man. He attended a one room school, while in high school played billiards with the local undertaker for a dime a point, and after two years at the U. of Illinois and two stops at Black Mountain College, traveled through the trans-mountain West following the winds of writing and employment. From 1965 to 1970 he lived in England, where he lectured at the U. of Essex. He has since lived and taught in Kansas, Chicago and San Francisco; throughout the 1980s he has taught in the Creative Writing Program of the U. of Colorado, Boulder, and, with his wife Jennifer Dunbar Dorn, edited the newspaper *Rolling Stock*. His major works include *The Newly Fallen, Hands Up!, Geography, Recollections of Gran Apacheria, Gunslinger, Hello La Jolla* and *Yellow Lola* (poetry), and *The Rites of Passage, Some Business Recently Transacted In the White World* and *The Shoshoneans* (prose).

DATE DUE

WITHDRAWN

	PRINTED IN U.S.A.